CONTINUED CASES

RICHARD HAGUE

DOS MADRES PRESS INC.
P.O. Box 294, Loveland, Ohio 45140
www.dosmadres.com   editor@dosmadres.com

Dos Madres is dedicated to the belief that the small press is essential to the vitality of contemporary literature as a carrier of the new voice, as well as the older, sometimes forgotten voices of the past. And in an ever more virtual world, to the creation of fine books pleasing to the eye and hand.

Dos Madres is named in honor of Vera Murphy and Libbie Hughes, the "Dos Madres" whose contributions have made this press possible.

Dos Madres Press, Inc. is an Ohio Not For Profit Corporation and a 501 (c) (3) qualified public charity. Contributions are tax deductible.

Executive Editor: Robert J. Murphy

Illustration & Book Design: Elizabeth H. Murphy
www.illusionstudios.net

Typeset in Adobe Garamond Pro & SF Comic Script
ISBN 978-1-953252-89-0
Library of Congress Control Number: 2023941691

First Edition
Copyright 2023 Richard Hague
All rights reserved. No part of this book may be reproduced or transmitted in any form or by any means graphic, electronic or mechanical, including photocopying, recording, taping or by any information storage or retrieval system, without the permission in writing from the publisher.
Published by Dos Madres Press, Inc.

For my writing communities

Writers Table of Originary Arts Initiative
Southern Appalachian Writers Cooperative
Northern Appalachian Writers Association
Writers Conference of Northern Appalachia
The Literary Club of Cincinnati
Poets Muddle Through

"Writing in the April 1904 issue of *The Atlantic* (sic), Whitman declared that he was tired of 'gloved gentleman words.' He admired 'unhemmed latitudes, coarseness, directness, live epithets, expletives, words of opprobrium, resistance.'"
—Dwight Garner,
"Mark My Words" *NYT Book Review*, Nov. 8, 2020

"The opposition is indispensable. A good statesman, like any other sensible human being, always learns more from his opponents than from his fervent supporters."
—Walter Lippman,
"The Indispensable Opposition"

"Our credo must be the exposure of the plunderers, the steerers, the wirepullers, the bosses, the brokers, the campaign givers and takers ... So I say: Stew, percolate, pester, track, burrow, besiege, confront, damage, level, care."
—Wayne R. Barrett, 1945-2017,
author of *Trump: The Greatest Show on Earth: The Deals, the Downfall, the Reinvention*, on his funeral prayer card

"Increasingly, I understand US. history as the history of debate, and our style of democracy as one that moves only through contest and challenge. We lament conflict and strife, but I think the lesson is that is exactly how we do and must do democracy.
—Martha Jones,
contributor to the 1619 Project

Facit indignatio versum. —Juvenal

◆ TABLE OF CONTENTS ◆

Introduction 1

▪ ON THE STREET ▪

Directions 7
HELL IS REAL 9
On Learning My Neighbor's Dog's Name Is "Fester" 11
The Tranquility Trials 12
Catiary 16
Xenia 17
How Long Ago The Heat 20
Finger: An Elegy In Eights 22
Decline of the Rake 23
Covid Diary 25
Song For St. Survivor 26

▪ IN SCHOOL ▪

Foiling Chat GPT 29
"I Have The Time" 31
In Vivid Sunlight, Becca 32
Lunch Poem 33
Where Are They And What Are They Doing There? 35
My Luddite Muse 37
Class Notes 38
Afternoon With A Young Poet 40

Why No Rhyme?..45
Walkiewicz Pitches Woo..46
Ab Sum 48
Virginity...49
Too Late 50
Wrinkled Face/"Wrinkled Fact"..51
"I'd Rather Be A Rich Hooker Than A Poor Poet"...............52
The Poetry Game 53
The Weirdest Poem Ever Quoted Hamlet............................54
Begin Egg & End Egg..55

▪ IN COUNTRY ▪

Horizontal Hydraulic Fracking..59
Under His Garden, The Sounds 60
Mr. MAGA Tours the Former Eden 61
Cool Free Market Capers...62
Limitless...63
Resistance, Or Our Most Worthy Habits 64
Men At Work..66
To Kiss A Train..67
The Air We Ate..68
What I Had Instead of Stories 69
Washed Out 70
What Is Worse...71
History of a Father 72
Characters For A Novel of the Days 75
Message from Frackingport 77
Also In America...78
Not All Sides Are Represented Here 81
Interrogation During The Old War 83
In The Time of Great Extinctions.......................................85
Unfinished To Do List...86

■ STATES OF THE ARTS ■

The Poem's Work: After Salman Rushdie	89
Squash Erotic	90
Elegy for Before, Behind, Between, Above, Below	92
After The Admonitions	94
Buenos Noches, Noches	96
The Professor Eats A Late Linguine	97
Acme Dream Removal	98
Vlad	100
Alternative Facts: The Primer	102
Come On	103
Steps in Defending One's Self From "Empowered Ignorance"	105
What Suits, You	108
The Capitol Grill	109
Hurt God	111
Beautiful	112
Soup To Nuts	113
Linnaeus Sniffs Around The Capitol	114
America	118
Marshal Law	120
The Inevitability of Sand	122
Pilgrims	123
Conduit	126
Notes	129
About the Author	133
Acknowledgements	135

INTRODUCTION

In 2009, Word Press published *Public Hearings*, my collection of "poems satirical, social, and political," as I termed them. The book was arranged in four parts: On The Street, In School, In Country, and States of the Arts. The reader will see that this book is organized in exactly the same way. I have suspected since *Public Hearings* that *Continued Cases* would be necessary. I was sadly confident that for ongoing absurdities, outrages, divisions, troubles, lies, distortions, weird subcultures, conspiracy theories, and general willingness to be fooled and foolish, a large swath of America is indeed exceptional, if not Great Again. Surely there would be subjects enough for further poems at a later date, time enough to gather more evidence. So these poems continue to be ongoing issues, unfinished business.

On the Street collects poems about and for the people, about street level cultural and political concerns not addressed in States of the Arts. Some of the poems are merely irreverent, some are deadly serious. In an article in the December 2019 *Atlantic*, Margaret Atwood is quoted from a speech she gave to Amnesty International: "Such material enters a writer's work, not because the writer is or is not consciously political, but because a writer is an observer, a witness, and such observations are the air he breathes." The poems in all the sections continue the complaints and protests and satire in *Public Hearings*: these too are hearings, gatherings of evidence, testimonies, many leading to what should be indictments, if not in the courts of law, then in the courts of conscience and in the grand juries of common sense, decency, and reasoned public opinion.

In School continues my sometimes frustrated and sometimes sympathetic responses to, and critiques of, the American educational culture and its perpetrators and victims as I encountered them in various high school classrooms from 1969 to 2014. I insist that my career among students was one mostly of stimulation, satisfaction, and joy, but when it came to some of the adults, I was often annoyed, occasionally enraged, and even sometimes stupefied, by their lack of common sense (and of their ignorance of valuable uncommon sense) about what teaching and learning could be and the courage to make over the system to promote a more effective, empowering, and joyful environment, the all-too rare excellent and inspiring administrators and teachers nothwithstanding. Great minds and sharp practitioners in and out of the classroom over a couple of centuries—Thoreau, Whitman, John Dewey, Lev Vygotsky, Jeanie Oakes, Theodore Sizer, to name just a few—have known how to practice education (and how not to), but the habit of repeating what doesn't work over and over still infected most of the American high school teaching establishment during the years these poems were prompted. It only got worse, I learned from some still in the classroom, as instruction during the pandemic was on-lined or devolved into "hybrids" that didn't work. (Look up the etymology of "hybrid "and see why not.) It is a dire case of arrested development, and it is a miracle that our students are not further behind than they are in relation to the rest of the world. Or maybe most of the world itself is wrong as well, and the higher scores of nations other than the US mean that everyone has capitulated to rote learning, STEM propaganda, and the for-profit, capitalist-imperialist intentions of the technocrats. Certainly the plague of climate change denial suggests that for all of humanity's best practices of education, something is direly amiss, Greta Thunberg the exception that proves the rule. All of the vast "developed" countries—the US, Russia, India, China—continue to mess our own nests, not to mention those of our fellow earthlings, and behave as if unable to figure out what to do, or to call upon the will to do it. There will be the occasions of many more warnings and lamentations as the crisis deepens.

In light of the various "realities" loose in our culture, I have foregone any attempt at creating a consistent tone in this collection. Some poems are flippant, some snarky, some brooding, some serious, some probably silly. To deal with all the manifestations of nonsense, vileness, and dunderheadedness that have run amuck over the years in which these poems have been written, any sort of stable emotional control is temporary, despite the claims of Learishly self-ignorant leaders. Now and then a small, lonely, nearly forsaken poem or two in any given section will remind us of how we might live better, of what we might grow to believe.

In Country refers to soldiers active overseas; here it is also intended to be taken literally as in the nation of the United States, or additionally, "in country," as in rural places, many of which have often been treated as sacrifice zones where mountain top removal and fracking, just to name two major enemies, have continued to overturn any and all respect for nature's laws and for rural justice. The voices speaking from such "flyover lands" have been infamously disregarded. Nature itself is talking back in this era of climate change and foolish, dangerous deregulation.

Just as there are now thousands of citizen scientists assisting in hundreds of important studies on the most local level, so I want to acknowledge and join the citizen poets, who at the local level pay attention to, offer witness, and advocate for right living and right thinking, in their towns and cities, their own regions. A fine example is the work of Cincinnatian Saad Ghosn, whose annual book-length gatherings of *For A Better World: Poems of Peace and Justice*, in which many of these first appeared, offers a model for the work of citizen poets and their editors. Just as there is the local food movement, this is an example of an equivalent and excellent local political poetry movement.

States of the Arts expands the meaning of "arts" to include not only what we generally understand the term to mean but as well the best and worst examples of governance, agriculture, general caretaking of the planet, technology, cultural traditions, and so on. It is the longest section in the book; such distorted practices, characters, and personalities require extended examination. As was demanded by his grieving wife about the life and work of her husband Willy Loman, that example of exhausted, hollowed-out, misinformed American values, "attention must be paid."

In a dream, Greta Thunberg appeared before me, demanding to know what I had done to make sure my own children would be aware of climate change, fascism, and willful ignorance. This book is part of my answer.

—RICHARD HAGUE
2023

ON THE STREET

Directions

Since you have become lost,
few options:
stay where you are,
strange constellations
lining up above you,
or hope for sea legs restored.
Dream up a redeemed Calypso
or gracious Siren who might find you,
save or conceal you.

Closer to home,
at the hollow sycamore,
turn towards where
some old man, maybe Adam,
lost his ax.
Pick it up, use it.
Much is in need of axing.

Make sure to avoid
low spots, old wells,
entrances to purgatory,
those yellow whiffs of sulfur.

When you think
you have found the way,
when you think you're there
and that everyone
is gathering to cheer,
remember the way
is never the way,

and it is always
long, often wrong,
and lonely.

Hell Is Real
billboard on southbound I-71, central Ohio

Pilgrims and patriots,
please notice to our left
six hundred thirty acres
of flatplate glaciated Creation
permanently deforested,
planted to monocultures
of GMO "corn" and "soybeans,"
fertilized with thousands of gallons
of petroleum-based,
war-ensured chemicals,
tamed by huge "Sodbusters,"
bastardized bulldozers.
Here tree lines are gone,
small creeks clogged,
ancient kames and moraines
wiped out by years
of plowing and compaction.
Here earthworms are extinct,

As soon may be
our saintly farmers,
these soft-bodied things
who move inside
the climate-controlled cabs
of their earth-breaking machines,

Who every Sunday
point their fingers and
build signs against sin,

which clearly thrives somewhere
else, and must be brought to
the attention
of all of us traveling,
they must presume,
from Sodom
to Gomorrah.

On Learning
My Neighbor's Dog's Name Is Fester

Not as good, I think, as my dead friend's
cats, "Dr. Todt" and "Plague,"
but close. Best in these times of
siloed memes of sappy
to hire some poet-namer
with a full case of despair
and bleak realism:
"Putrid." "Scab." "Rabies."

Call your hound named "Mange"
at the dog park, loudly, often.
Gross out the honey-minds
and cute-sick among the gapers.

Too much fake news in the world of pets.
So give us a break: How about
"Catarrh" the cat? "Maggot" the mouse.
How about "Kneecap," the Irish wolfhound?

The Tranquility Trials

> *feeling nervous, irritable, or on edge*
> *having a sense of impending danger, panic or doom*
> *difficulty concentrating*
> *having trouble sleeping*
>
> —from Signs and Symptoms of General Anxiety Disorder, Anxiety & Depression Association of America

1.

At first, most suspected the weather: strange, yellow hurricanes full of hair and sour bird-like tweets from the watery sinks of Florida. Swamps increased. In the nation's Capitol, gluts of gobbledygook flowed from the seats of the Cabinet like slow oil spills. Crooks donned priests' robes and heard the confessions of Coal and Gas, forgiving all. Mobsters chewed on pages of the Constitution. Children began to shiver for no apparent reason. Parents awoke hungry and cold at night.

2.

Jail cells appeared in random villages, filled with dark-haired infants. Far away, mothers in moaning lines emptied their pockets, looking for names and addresses. With cheap whiskey, officials fought off the dread brought on by the kidnappings. Long sessions of self-incrimination convened in bus stations, parish halls, and neighborhood polling places. Convictions lagged. The words *wall* and *fence* and *border* and *barrier* scrambled across the floor of Congress like cockroaches. Under the benches of the Supreme Court, cold shadows gathered like flood water. Screams of rape and abandonment and despair slithered through them like snakes.

3.

Indictments showed up like parking tickets on the windshields of lawyers, bishops, cooks, mechanics, senators. Bus drivers slammed their doors on workers. Uber drivers menaced riders with Glocks. Anyone who walked was soon limping. Stores ran out of toothpaste. The air turned gray and metallic. The lungs of people who had smoked all their lives began to bleed. Nuns complained of invisible hands under their habits, fondling their buttocks. Everything red turned yellow and blue collapsed into black. Rivers dried up. Insects grew scarce. Toads disappeared. Stories began to be told.

4.

And so legislation was forced through to throttle the newspapers, whose staffs staggered into the dividers of interstates like Okies without trucks. Dust devils swept up birth certificates and cigarette lighters. An a capella singing group named Mr. Happy and His Laughing Apostles were abducted from Columbus, Ohio to Silver City, New Mexico, where they were buried up to their necks in sand. Almost half the population of grandmothers died within four days. The stories continued.

5.

And so the government shut down from Groundhog Day to Halloween, opening only to pay a few hundred of itself, and then shut down again. McDonald's went out of business. Starbuck's. Two thousand small craft breweries. Wall Street saboteurs tossed rolls of paper towels to men in suits. Rescue dogs guarded the doors of abandoned asylums. Magazines now came with voices (synthesized Lucille Ball, Carol Channing, a very old Leonard Cohen) so they could be listened to with eyes closed. There were lots of closed eyes. Implantation of government-issue personal chips began in kindergarten. Robins, starlings, English sparrows, and pigeons disappeared. Large angers of feral cats sneaked around major cities. Electricity began to taste sour. Epidemics: sudden tooth loss, visual migraines, night-time itching.

6.

Thus emergency measures were adopted, desperate times calling for desperate measures. The foot was shortened by an inch and a half. A pound no longer weighed a pound. Five cents were three cents. Riots in the streets were the occasions of laughter and folding chairs. Hospitals handed out switchblades. Only those whose names ended in P were allowed to stay in Washington. Whales swam far up the Potomac and died. New books were forbidden. Roving bands of goon squads wore bright yellow letters on their jackets that spelled out "GOON." Most calories were now in the form of corn syrup. All surgeons banned from the Emergency Rooms, minor government officials instead read propaganda pamphlets to the sick and injured on "Patience" and "Kindness" from noon until five o'clock. No one said "Mexico" anymore. "Please" and "Thank you" didn't make it into the new dictionary. Night seemed twice as long. The screaming never stopped.

7.
Over the Marcellus and Utica shales, toilets began to fill with hellish sludge. Misspellings quadrupled. Peacemakers were rounded up and executed on the fields of football stadiums. Social security cards burst into flames in the pockets and purses of retirees. Congress voted for More Din and Big Litter. Sergeant Chaos and Private Parts became sit-com stars. Elections were cancelled. At night, there were no stars. During the day, even at noon, it was always sunset.

CATIARY

> *We estimate that free-ranging domestic cats kill 1.3–4.0 billion birds and 6.3–22.3 billion mammals annually, and that un-owned cats cause the majority of this mortality.*
> —*Nature Communications*, Jan 29, 2013

In this neighborhood of cars and chop-shops,
Glocks and ammo, a hundred garages
and fly-by-night oil change joints,
cats the color of rust or dumped engine oil
lurk and dart through alleys
of city wilderness, hell's menagerie.
Everywhere, song sparrows die
the slow death, mauled and flung by
tabbies, calicos, seal points gone feral
as ocelots. On porches,
food arrayed in pet bowls beside the bannisters,
Maine Coon-scarred possums ascend to burgle
kibbles and bits and moldy flakes of tuna;
slugs thick as fingers clench coughed-up hairballs;
nighthawks beep madly across a Cheshire frown of moon.

Xenia

> *But here is a poor homeless man,*
> *and you must look after him.*
> —Princess Nausicaa, *The Odyssey*, Book VI, 8th Century BCE

You may have seen him—
   friend, father, brother, son—
at Vine and Elder, Over-The-Rhine,
   brightfaced in late winter
low-west light,
   beard gray-gold and sparse
as Ithaka's scraggly wheat.
   Now empty bottles glint
in the gutter like
   wave-washed, wine-dark stones, and
the shades of his dead comrades
   stumble and moan
in piss-stinking doorways
   while he does not sleep,
still lion-like in the watchfulness
   of officer and survivor.

His arrival in our city?
   Washed ashore, unconscious,
at the Public Landing,
   he crawled up granite cobbles,
coughing oily water,
   eyes burning.
              Police were called:
they smelled wine on his breath
   (the last of bottles he'd scavenged
behind a Pittsburgh 7-Eleven

    to share with his thirsty crew)
and he was unshaven;
    nor would he tell them his name.
When they roughed him up
    he blurted, I am *Everyman*, I am *Nobody,*
so they punched him.
                      Into a squad car
they finally hustled him, silent
    where he had been thrown,
then to the Justice Center,
    fingerprinted
(to no avail—not in the system,
    no more than Laestrygonians),
told to strip and shower
    then dressed in coarse clothes
(offered no oil, no soft hands
    of servants to soothe him,
no banquet in his honor
    where he could tell his tale,
name his father,
    recount his great adventures)—
rather, he was smacked and shackled,
    bum-rushed, cursed, made sad sport of,
then, in cold and wind,
    thrown back on the street,

Because we have forgotten
    the ancient wisdom, the deeply
human way: help poor
    strangers, outlanders,
pilgrims: offer *xenia*,
    "hospitality,"

because our distressed,
    our homeless, our
unfortunate and lost,
    all "pale forms
fainting at the door"
    may well be heroes,
gods, prophets, saviors, and we must
    welcome them among us
or suffer wraths and ruins,
    the "mechanisms of
enforcement" by which
    we forfeit friends,
heaven, justice, earth, our souls.

How Long Ago The Heat
during the so-called Cold War

Our backyard fifty-gallon drum
was mostly rust,
red-orange pulses of flame
lancing its sides
as my father fed it
cereal boxes and newspapers,
fading V-Day victory columns
corrected to smoke in seconds.

Everything was eligible:
an old catcher's mitt, moldy,
ripped, its stench a burning dog.
Once, a stake of polished
wood, a piano leg, whose
lacquered brilliance burst into fumes
that stung my eyes.

Burning was as common as breathing,
and what would not burn
the first time flung in
would wait, soak up rain,
dry out in sun, crumple and shrink,
then join stampeding flames
when lit again.

How much poison we must
have created, how many
future heat waves, floods, dry spells:
paint cans, old galoshes,

early plastic junk,
transistor radios,
Cracker Jack gizmos
boys quickly broke
and tossed.

High on our switch-backed
ridge where the city
garbage trucks couldn't climb,
we joined the steel mills
over the hill, our
daily backyard conflagrations
a rhyme with open hearths
below—
our hot messes,
our tributary blazes
that for generations smote the air
and threw such smoke
that even the stars
went extinct at night.

Finger: An Elegy In Eights
Junedale Meat Market, Steubenville, Ohio, 1963

Hours later, we found it in
the hamburger trimmings, nail still
intact, its few thick dark hairs stiff-
standing. Like half-drunk knuckleheads,
we matchboxed it, wrapped that in brown
butcher paper, addressed *To Gene*
with no return. I pushed it through
the slot myself.
                    It never got
to him: full lost, for months somewhere
in our bleak, raw, dismembered world,
undelivered, shunted here/there,
it stiffened, stank, and rotted, his
name all over it, his print still
whorled like Braille into its mute blind
end, which pointed down, toward Hell.

Decline of the Rake
clearly not *after Hogarth*

It helped him
clear the winter mulch
this morning, making way
for Lacinato kale.
But he should have known—
its tracks in soil
were hyena's stripes,
bear claws mauling
spruce bark.

He thought it just
a tool, at his command,
but in his plague-time's poisoned
furor, it got out of hand,
dark agent of its own use
(he tried to tell himself) so
came down upon a mole
that flailed across the driveway,
thus stabbed to death in light.

No going back from such sudden
dread epiphanies—tool by tool,
object by object,
vote by vote,
much turns ill.

Hell is such
wicked transformation—
treason of the innocent and real,

delusions of intention:
a lie is now the truth,
morning's dew is acid rain,
every cloud a nuke
dropped on a synagogue,
every hour of attempted sleep
a restless vivid purgatory
to survive.

Covid Diary

The day of the long rain.
The day of not enough to read.
The day of eating six times.
The day of prostration on the day bed.
The day-doses of medicine.
The day of day-old leftovers.
The day of no appointments whatsoever.
The day of couched paralysis.
The day of slight recovery near cocktail time.
The day of *blahblah* cable tv.
The day of aggravating the cat on my lap.
The day of no doctor.

The day of death counts climbing.
The day of bankruptcies among the poor.
The day of bad headlines.
The day of old socks.
The day of graylight, followed by useless sunshine,
then long rain again and then long rain.
Then another day just like that one.
Then another one.

Another.

Song For St. Survivor

You did not starve when famine visited the land.
Somehow, you fattened, orchidic,
feeding on suffering and air.
Your flesh grew veined with light,
your words layered, fragrant as onions.
Nor did you weep over death
nor count your losses,
nor harbor resentments.
You did not rend your garments, gnash your teeth.

You did not judge or take revenge.
You rarely prayed,
and then, never in supplication,
but always in thanksgiving:

For the spotted newt,
for the embossed and brassy-eyed toad,
for the grace of the grass snake,
the vast wealth of termites.

You did not hoard your smiles
but distributed them like fishes and loaves,
loving the sound of crowds.

Never was a word
you never said.
Always, you sang,
always.

IN SCHOOL

Foiling Chat GPT

In whatever you write—laundry lists, poems, mocking
bitter screeds, chaste autofictions—
mention your hometown unexpectedly,
i.e. "In *Moby-Dick*, Melville's greatest achievement,
we are faced with an existential crisis of male power,
symbolized by the enormously phallic Steubenville, OH."

Make sure to include the word
"supercalifragilisticexpialidocious"
in your pamphlet on
sexually transmitted diseases.

Mispell "misspell" in every chapter
of your graphic novel about
teaching English as a second language.

Write dozens of sonnets with maybe twelve or
eleven lines of, like, oh, approximately, 127 syllables.

Sign every letter of protest you write
against homelessness with the name
Donald J. Trump.

Insist the phrase "patently liquid"
appear in your report on Mt. Everest.

Sign every petition to end gun violence
you are offered
Donald J. Trump.

Threaten to pull the plug, repeating this threat
for two thousand lines.

Sign every tax return you fudge
Donald J. Trump.

Skip one important in
any legal document you compose.

Do such things to
remain original, skeptical, safe,
yourself, and just.

End anything you write
with the world "salad."

Salad.

"I Have The Time"
—a young student declares cheerfully

So do I, I answer—but
it is the dark, bleeding Time,
garish as a hooked chinook,
gills flared fire,
flesh a cold struggle
of crimson strangling.
It is not the flimsy, small-time Time
half-alive like a little insect
in an idle office full of the stink
of burned coffee,
nor the impatient foot-stomping
wait at the diesel-poisoned bus stop.
The Time I have has been worked over,
rode hard, put up wet.
It groans to catch its own breath.
It hasn't got time for messing around.
Mornings, it hop-alongs ahead of me,
dropping notes from its
fleeing saddle-bags:
     Hurry up
 Loser
   You're dead

In Vivid Sunlight, Becca

Heraclitus opens the shades

In vivid sunlight, Becca,
slashed by Venetian swords of fire,
dives into a blast of words.

She is gone, her glasses
flying atoms or bees of fire,
even the letters of her name

floating like scintilla, motes. Fire
burns everything in the room, fire
turns the dullest words

into flaming gases,
window-panes to orange-purple spurts of words
—fire, words, glasses—

even in vivid sunlight, Becca.

Lunch Poem

Today we're writing lunch poems.
To keep from doing it,
he talks to anyone around him about even the stupidest things:
lipstick, the Cleveland Browns, how to make a cheat sheet,
and when teacher tells him even *that* could be a poem,
making a cheat sheet,
he laughs.

To keep from writing poems,
she rubs lotion on her hands for half an hour,
turning them over and over like Lady Macbeth
until they feel as slippery as catfish.
Slippery, teacher says, *that* could be a poem,
and she laughs.

To keep from writing poems,
he daydreams about Las Vegas,
about hitting it rich in a casino,
but when he reaches into his pocket,
all he really has is eleven cents.
Poor as teacher he thinks,
and he laughs.

To keep from writing poems,
she listens to Antonio talk, talk,
talk, talk, talk, talk, talk
until it drives her crazy,
and when the teacher says *that* could be a poem,
things that drive you crazy,
she laughs.

To keep from writing poems,
he acts like he's really writing but secretly
he's thinking about his cousin
and the little dog he had
that ate a lamp, a boot, and part of a dead pony.
But that's weird, he thinks, teacher would latch onto it.
So he stops.

To keep from writing poems,
she spends the whole class inventing the best lunch ever,
and then, in her imagination,
she sits right down and eats it, every bit.
And then she belches, and when teacher says
that's the poem, ready to get out,
she laughs.

And then the poem, like an echo
across the room,
laughs too.

Where Are They And What Are They Doing There?

After keeping count in workshops and seminars over a couple of years—this time 12 girls and 1 boy in a poetry workshop, Abingdon, VA.

Are they out in the sun
thinking of riffles, catfish, big cars
with engines that roar like sauropods
at the touch of a foot?

Or are they at the bottoms of lakes,
swimming naked in blue-green cold
where their fathers' ghosts
lurk like drowned stumps
beneath the gaudy bodies of such sons?

What worries us is this:
they are not here, the boys,
working up shacks or tree houses of words,
building boats of memories and poems.
They are not among us
riding motorcycle lives
that speed off the end of the page.

Only we are here,
girl-women breaking
the fasts of our silences,
arriving at Nativities of words,
but missing something, worried about them,
and so inventing places for them to be,
poems, plays, slim novels

for those boys,
speaking lives they can come home to,
laughing, ready, irreplaceable—
brothers, cousins, husbands.

My Luddite Muse

In the middle of writing class, all of them variously hunched
and squinting, notebooks square before them like

altar settings at the christening of Verb, someone's iPhone shrills
over the murmur of pens on paper. For a moment

I listen, hoping it might be the muse, her liquid melody
arriving to set honey even in the cells of letters they form:

there, in a capital O, a tenth of a thimble
of ambrosian clarity, there, in some peaceful small-case

unomi-like *u*, a honeyed sip. But no: tinny, plastic-
sounding, it is immediate distraction, dry annoyance.

So I invoke better: a scarlet violin appears in the hands of a wild
sophomore: she saws at it, grinning, cutting our silence

into rough-hewn logs we lash together with words,
a great raft of song upon which, rapt as sirened Odysseus,

we set out, far past Troy and Sandy Pylos,
toward the enchanted isles of Nophonia, where

we'll drift into endless adventure, unreachable,
no thoughts of ever coming back.

Class Notes

My head leaning back
in the lecture hall,

the professor droning
for two unbroken hours on the

Great Germanic Consonant Shift,
(I bleed, I suffer, I moan)

I see, far above me,
crisp asteroids

stuck to the ceiling tiles,
constellations of white

semispheres of chewed
and spittled paper:

shredded sheets
from unsuccessful essays,

lover's break-up notes,
forged Oxycontin

scripts: constellations of woe,
dry Orions of misfortune.

—If only we could as easily
spit out our troubles,

something of the farewell kiss in them,
so heavenward and so finally

that they could never
fall back down upon us:

*Adios, you little
suckers, so long.*

Afternoon With Young Poet

1. The Poem Arrests His Attention

He's sitting on his porch doing nothing,
all day doing nothing, just hangin, chillin,
chillin so long he's breathless,

stiff. Just about done in,
doing nothing.
So the poem swerves around the

corner, lights flashing, hits
the curb, jumps
out before its iambic's finally stopped,

storms up the steps, shouts,
"What you doing, boy!"
And the boy says, "Nothin."

"Exactly!" the poem shouts, and
writes him up a ticket, five hundred dollars,
"Idling and loafing

away a life, wasting a gift
that requires action and fine words
plus thanksgiving."

His sentence? "Look at a hundred
insects in the museum,
imagine their indigo and emerald and

iridescent lives.
Taste moo shu pork
with someone you've just met

and over dinner memorize
her life story. Kiss someone you've hoped
to love, despite your weakness and fear.

Love your teacher, though he is
balding and red-faced and angry
some of the time, for he

has treasure and wealth to
splurge on you
in the name of Beauty."

2. *Why He Needs Beauty*

If he doesn't get it,
he will die. Just as surely as a starved child
wastes away, he will

fade away into squalor and ugliness,
the daily assault of advertising and prejudice,
the interior poisoning of good will,

the rotting away of happiness and worth,
the month always longer than the check,
the pantry empty,
the roaches of poverty scrabbling his pillow.

Beauty costs nothing,
comes with every dawn, every moment of keen
perception in the subway, like Pound's

The apparition of these faces in the crowd—
petals on a wet, black bough

every noticing, like Basho's, of how

the distant mountains
are reflected in the eye
of the dragonfly

Beauty is toughness,
goodness, the way out of anger
and the smothered mine
of self.

He needs beauty like he needs air,
food, love, the touch
of the world firing his nerves,

the pull of gravity making
him strong even as he
struggles uphill
against it.

3. Four Questions He Had, With Answers

Why is there smoke?

Because all that burns
is body, even splintered wood,
even curling leaves, spilled oil—and
smoke is what body always says
when heat comes near.

Are all the elephants dead?

No. Thousands of elephants
survive in the dreams
of beautiful children
in the inner cities.

All night, the elephants
crowd out the sirens and policemen,
the crack and Glocks,
the crying and hating,
making room
for the jungle filled
with the sound of
xylophones.

Is it fair?

Usually. But even
when it's not, we
must be patient.
Eventually, it all comes

around again
on the guitar.

Why yellow?

Because the universe
is mostly electricity,
and everyone
hits its switch.

Why No Rhyme?
a student inquires

Vomit, for example, or compost. Sure, the bird
has two wings, one rhyming with the other, making flight,

but not everything is an eagle. Amoebas,
for example. Shapeshifters rule: light, neutrons,

gravity—waves or particles? It depends.
Not everything is wrapped tight, static,

always in place. The weather for example: one day
tornado, the next day calm. Even the continents

wander and transform. For example, mutations,
the axolotl. Shit happens. But rhyme implies

order, regularity— in these monkey-minded days
almost certain desperation—a lie.

Walkiewicz Pitches Woo

after the mispronunciation of "wanton"
in a recitation of Marvell's "To His Coy Mistress"

1.

In the wonton fields of his
fine Chinese dream,
Sam winds up;
it is May,
birds melodious as madrigals
in the woods
beyond the river,
and Sam
continues to wind up;
the air warm,
and she willing,
that nameless beauty
reclining in the wonton fields,
heated as sesame oil,
juicy as dim sum,
her hair dark and rich as hoisin sauce,
her lips full sweet and sour,
and Sam winds up,
ready,
and pitches
woo.

2.

She, of course, is coy.
She resists, lovely
in her resistance,
even as Sam

revs and revs
and winds up;
she will not swing
at any pitch of his,
nor Woo's,
nor Lee's,
not Chin's—
certainly not this
Walkiewicz's—
that's a mouthful
she won't chew.

3.

So in the wonton fields
of youth and love,
Walkiewicz pitches woo
to she who will not be wooed,
(nor Walkiewieczed)
and though he winds and revs,
revs and winds,
he's getting nowhere:

So it is with all such swains,
forever young, forever fair
(except when bunting foul),
and all remember their failed love,
how sad it is, how ill, as
when poor Walkiewicz
that sad day
tried to pitch some woo.

AB SUM

She has not come, again,
to Latin class, her hair
sweet conjugations
of bronze and light,
her hands the sleek ferrets
of our desire.
Fr. Majewski takes roll,
the Polish slant of his voice
tipping us overseas every
morning, as if we are travelers
approaching some fogged-in
dock, listening into the distance
for however his voice
might lighthouse us ashore.

Her bare knees
have stirred and parted
to the press of my palms,
her breath
has wandered the hair of my wrists,
the small of her slender, hot
back has berthed briefly
in the trembling harbor
of my skin.

But this morning
Father speaks her name,
looks up, turns absently
toward me
in a silence like departure,
then speaks it again, slowly,

and again.

Virginity

It has been born to
blush, drinks warm
milk, stores its socks
neatly in the proper
places.
        O it is
as large a thing
as mountains or oceans,
or the insect population of
all the air.
        It is
velvet touching itself,
silk whispering its
untold story, revealing
nothing.
        It is ready
but not willing. It is
not cocked, unfired.
        Near its end,
it is a book
splayed open
to the introduction,
and beside it,
on the bed stand,
a nervous cigarette
swooning up sultry
tangoes in afternoon's
martinied light.

Too Late

She does not open
the book her father
has given her: *A Teen's
Guide To Postponing
Sexual Involvement*,
its title clunky
as some boy's first fumbling
at her bra straps
in the dark.
The book sits gleaming,
dense, flat as a creek rock
under water
in her bedside lamp's
dim illumination.
Its interior,
she imagines,
is like a geode's,
sharp with crystalline rules,
injunctions, imperatives,
or like a stream's rocky bottom
littered with bedsprings,
broken bottles, tires,
stripped negligees.
She feels water rising
past her ankles,
tepid socks
tugged downward.
Then things seem to swim
between her thighs,
slick brightnesses
that might well not
be fish.

Wrinkled Face/"Wrinkled Fact"

In this case, "t" for "e."
O, professor, typos are signs
something knows better
than we do
that much or all
is amiss:
sum thing tallies our little bumbles
into vast body counts.

Abed, in the depths of slip,
we dream wyrd trips
we might not wake
from:

night? nacht? nichts?

"I'd Rather Be A Rich Hooker Than A Poor Poet"

He says this when I call him
a point whore for wanting
everything he writes
to be graded. "It is not
a for-pay transaction," I
tell him. "Poetry is not
a product, but a process,
a way of being."

"To hell with it," he says,
"that's just what I mean."

The Poetry Game

1.

Snatch the orange from sunset
and paint it on the tiger.
Pour dirty water into a clear sock
and call it amoeba.
Stalk the edges of dreams
armed with the dictionary of Triumph.
Poetry plays this game.

2.

The noun is humped by the verb
in a hot, moist, adjectival dark.
Nine lines later the sport
is born, the freak with shark's teeth
and a Ph.D., a chimera hipping
hula hoops atop a pyramid.
Poetry plays this game.

3.

In the imagination, a great empty hall
that smells like a cathedral.
There ought to be incense
seething along its stone walls.
Somebody lifts her pen
and music begins.
Poetry plays this game.

The Weirdest Poem Ever Quoted Hamlet

It lay alone all its life
unloved, a virgin of
absolute zero. Even its
fingers fluttered when
kissed by its dreams, even its
hair, when touched by its demon
lover, sublimed away
like ice. At last
its final atom drifted
off, white period
in a blizzard.
The rest, it said,
is silence

Begin Egg & End Egg: From The Prompt

"Eggzactly vat it is you are
lookink for?" the professor
cried, a caricature
in German. It was late, he'd
been sleeping. Big noise
woke him. Into his study
he'd stepped to see
a great black figure
rummaging his waste basket,
tossing papers like a tornado.

When it turned
to face the professor,
it swelled to the size
of a small asteroid
and glowed. All was
not well. The house
trembled. Outside,
night, fleeing, glanced over its
shoulder like an accomplice.

The professor spluttered
more questions, took up
his book,
beat the intruder
down. It shrank
like a deflating
toad. It rolled up
tight, armored and silver

as a pangolin. It cursed
in Greek and
Lithuanian. All was
not well. The Professor
choked, his heart
churning. White settled
over his face
like a fresh napkin.

Life ate its last
snack and left, nothing
on the plate but
crumbs, a few grains
of salt,
the peeled shell
of an egg.

IN COUNTRY

Horizontal Hydraulic Fracking

Mark how the words themselves
are armed with lances, spikes,
towers, derricks, sickles, shivs,
self-pocked with the dead-on-bull's-eye-
poking punctuation of dotted *i*'s.

Language indicts itself;
bad words (and deeds) will out:

The *H*'s are squeezing, braced, land-
wrenching. That *z* is a wicked
switchback full of danger.
The *r*'s running through
are drill bits hot
at the gates of Hell.

They'll get there.
They'll take us with them.

Under His Garden The Sounds

Upright for a moment
in his plot, hoe at rest
beside him, he is startled
to see his own
shadow armed,
faceless brave with a spear
as long as himself, pointed darkness
inclined toward his neighbor's
innocent porch.

Deep in the earth,
under lakes, gulfs,
towns, oceans,
under groceries and high schools
and K-Marts,
a dull machinery groans.
The sun inspires bombs.
Rain is a wash of poison,
soil a sordid bivouac.
Water from faucets
bursts into flame.

All day he has sought
to grow beans; all day,
somewhere deeply near,
it seems always a time
of battle.

Mr. MAGA Tours The Former Eden

Ain't no way this rose
is real, and the color
of it—fake news. And
that Shasta daisy—
floozie, show-off, primadonna.
I'd say give me that
sulk of poison ivy
under the camellias,
that snakelet of ground ivy
across the back lawn.
I'll take that sprizz
of nettles in the zinnias—
and hell, I love that bindweed,
the way it'll trip up any wannabe Boss,
crawl up any Queen's or First Lady's dress.

Cool Free Market Capers

Third graders fall from
school windows,
computers like millstones
around their necks.
Instead of bandaging,
pale aides
prod heir broken bodies
with bar-coded answers
to online tests.
Venture capitalists look quickly
away, their consciences
at last grown heavy
as their wallets.

Blood congeals
in tiny pools
inside video games.
Handguns sprout from
the foreheads of babies.
In the state capitals.
unions,
as if cockroaches,
are stomped
by hundreds
of elected feet.

Limitless

after C.K. Williams' "The Nail"

Having recently recovered
from Carolyn Forché's "The Colonel"—
that sack of human ears,
that casual inhumanity—
I trip now over this,
headlong into pain and
brutality, the "grief
that is limitless."

And I imagine that grief,
need to speak and name it,
and it spews out of me, out of us,
beyond all saving edges,
past the tiny counties
of empathy and sorrow,
past the civil precincts of cities,
past the quiet borders of peace
and love,
past even the now hopeless
atmosphere.

It is pandemic,
a rocket of grief
with unlimited fuel
whose target is everywhere,
everyone,
its guidance
the code of our own DNA.

Resistance, Or, Our Most Worthy Habits
re: Scott McClanahan's dismissal of "the Appalachian Minstrel Show" and J.D. Vance's "elegy" for hillbilly culture

When anywhere, even in Rome,
we did as mountaineers would do.
When told to stay inside the lines,
we organized the strike.
When instructed to take our medicine,
we dug ginseng, ran naked in a blizzard.
When told to straighten up and fly right,
we crouched, veered left,
slid on our asses down the holler.
When told to listen up,
we clawhammered, fast,
and sang them down.
When counseled to lighten up,
we hoarded still-copper, scrap iron, bullet lead.
When told to get real,
we remembered Jack and Old Fire Dragaman
and dreamed up wilder worlds.

When ordered to chill,
we stoked interior fires.
When threatened with arrest,
we clogged beyond their reach.

At prayer, we profaned.
In profanity, we blessed.
In silence, we exhorted.
In poverty, we grew rich.

When silenced,
we became mountain streams
announcing imminent danger.
When nailed down,
we erupted like exploding stills.

Despite brief collaring and cuffing,
we slip our bonds and occupy lost days—
quoting Bible and Mother Jones,
and become gagging, hair-balling cats on
Matewan bloody pillows, mean dogs
gnawing Blankenship-guilty bones.

Men At Work
—mill towns in old Appalachia

In a clatter of collapsed beams,
bent steel, smashed masonry, gravity piling on,
cranes and derricks grub rubble with crab-clawed
buckets, plumbing the wreckage.
They raise a dark diesel racket.
Smashed lockers, open hearths, chemical tanks,
office-sheaves of nulled contracts tumble and spill,
each crane's new hoisting leaking down-gyves
of falling debris. Smoke lurks. Dust billows.
Angle iron squawls and contorts. Hell
has come.
                But then, exactly at noon,
workers crawl out of their high machines
or rusting crow's nests of scrap
and ladder down to flat remains
to break out lunch buckets and thermoses.
Hardhats cast aside, they flip on their MAGA ballcaps.
After, they smoke leisurely in the wreckage,
as if disaster is a daily event, no more surprising
than a ringing phone, as if ruin is their native landscape,
mountains of junk and rubble,
valleys of veed girders and tangled wire,
landscapes of waste and loss,
forests of burned metal through which small streams
of coolant and steaming seepage from custodians' closets
and wrecked break-room vending machines
trickle steadily downward,
fishless, toxic, all the wrong colors
for sky, or water, or blood.

To Kiss A Train

Weirton Junction WV, late Sixties,
Vietnam already eating his friends and cousins,
he worked summers on the railroad,
the Scrap Job, feeding the steel mills that fed the war
wrecked metal of all kinds—
trailers, skewed girders of burn-downs,
torched-off cartops and truck frames,
dismembered transmissions, their gears
broken off like blasted-out teeth.
All was digested by open hearth fire
so hot it napalmed away the dark
along Harmon Creek's black shores.

Then, one hungover night,
at the far end of the Scrap Yard,
at the foot of a gob pile blocking the moon,
he leaped from a crush of broom sedge and wild hemp,
a million pounds of diesel and steel
bearing down on him,
and offered his face.

The Air We Ate

The air we ate tasted of iron ore,
ten-penny nails, gutter sand.
Tardidgrades were our cousins in survival.
Our sneezes clattered like kicked trashcans.
Our tears were cinders and clinkers,
as if we wept grit or kidney stones. But weep

We didn't often, because we were
tough guys and our air, by god,
was the worst in the country. And daily
on high school tracks and cracked sidewalks
we ran and leaped, our lungs
blackening like the acid-rained
towers of churches.
Years later, when doctors warned us

Of "nodules" on our chest x-rays,
we snorted. Sure enough, doc,
they're pieces of rust and metal,
the air we sucked and chewed.
So much that some of us
still swear we're magnetic,
able to make our ways back like
homing pigeons
half a wrecked world off course.

What I Had Instead of Stories

"the dark jubilating Isaiah of mill and smoke marrow."
—James Wright, on my hometown

The ones I tell and have told for years
I made up. In a place whose history
is that its history will be lost,
there were no stories:
noisy town, railroads, steel mills—
cacophonies and cinders.
Old men and women hardly had voices.
The hills no longer spoke tongues.
I couldn't hear myself breathe,
and so any love I might have learned,
any grief I might have had to swallow,
any hope I might have had to dream up:
throw it out and turn away, boy, turn away.

And why wouldn't I, the air so bad
it was famous? Safer to suck in and hold
what I had to tell for later, when I could
hide in my future and testify
on paper, out of their sight and hearing.

I never wanted to say bad about my town,
except when I did. Even then, no regrets.
Everything, even the bad, I knew,
would go up in smoke.

Washed Out

My grandmother scrubbed the front porch
floor weekly. Old steam engines pounded three doors
down the street and raised a hell of dust. She was a good
Catholic woman, so swept and swabbed as well as she could
at what looked evil, like the spots on the soul
ancient nuns had taught her as a girl. But her husband

drove one of those iron horses, let it wheeze
on a downstreet siding when he stopped for lunch, its coal soot
seeping thickly from the smokestack.

Nothing stayed clean. The word *immaculate*
only appeared in catechisms.
Grit was another name for air.

What is Worse

> *"Following the splashes of blood wandering over the world"*
> —Galway Kinnell, "The Bear"

What if there is no blood?
In the air, no hum of bees or dragonflies?
No slink of minnows in the chromium stream?
What if soon there is no earned and painful death,
just "an etherized patient upon a table,"
being now the earth,
and weather becomes punishment—
rain, fire, wind the names of enemies
of our own invention?

Still the small thunder of jets high up,
bombs gorging their billion-dollar innards,
still the stink-hiss of traffic on the stalled rivers of asphalt,
still the diesel hymns of freight trains hauling parts of the land
to other parts of the land in the grand displacement,
the breaking mix, the moil.

How long I have been a part of it.
How long my comfort has cost the world.
Almost everything is, at last, smoke of my fires,
ash of my habits, fumes
of my heartless demands,
swirled over the embers of the world
from my greed's arrogant thurible.

And what if my hands still seem clean, nothing to wash guiltily off:
no sign warning *The End is Near* at the end of the road
I have bum-rushed my life along?

History of a Father

1: The Contents of His Pockets

A handful of shagbark hickory
nuts rattled in his right
front pocket whenever he entered
the house. One might think
him a country boy, bumpkin
with free lunch close
at hand. Wrong. In his left
pocket, tiny knives,
no longer than hornets,
their blades covered in
dried blood. One might think
him some sort of serial
murderer, on quite
a small scale. Wrong.
In his right back pocket,
his hand rested flat
against his own butt,
ready to whip quickly out
and smack me
to the floor.

2: The Last Voyage of His Shoes

If the concussion is intense
enough, a miner
may be blown from
his tied boots
         so that they
seem still to contain
his feet, one slightly

forward of the other,
                        as if
he is stepping toward
something curious,
strange—and he is,
                        that little curl
of gas unseen and unsmelled
that will instantly swell
and ignite and fill
his whole
world to the ceiling
with unbreathable
light.

3: *End Shift*

Grief was thus a
hard bargain: mixed
with guilt over
relief that the hand
would never strike
me again
             was the softening
joy of deliverance
after a hard youth
of ice and cold and
dusty cursing
and blood.
                Then, just
beyond the tipple
at the end of town,
a song sparrow, obscure in
fern and bramble,

its three clear
notes then spill
of song,
announced in me
a slow and small
forgiveness
for which I now
rehearse.

Characters For A Novel Of The Days

Mostly, days sauntered by
like strangers come on Saturday
to the county seat:
there'd be Wednesday,
t-shirted, bearded, smoking a Bugler he'd rolled
himself, thinking of squirrels and the mighty football team
of Beallsville. Or Monday would show up,
brooding by the soldier's monument
before the Monroe County Court House,
three June turkeys he'd bagged
under the game warden's radar
stashed like Ice Age boulders in his freezer.
Or there'd be Columbus Day,
bears loping across the fairground of her mind
as one did in a front-page photo
last autumn in the *Monroe County Beacon*.

Summer solstice passed the time
jawing about weather, jobs,
Mr. Piatt's garden,
Huff's new Charolais,
Jim Winland's hanging mole.

And there were days marvelous
as photographs of heaven:
the splashed litter of a robin's nest
flecked with blue shell,
strewn hagiography of wing and escape;
or sky after a sunset storm,
remembering the colors of last night's fire;

or the abrupt heartbreak of a hornet
landed harmless and beautiful on his knee,
or washed stones glimpsed sidelong
in some sandy palm of the creek,
or one noctilucent cloud
above the shadow poplar
like a moonless night's bright idea.

And some were strange, dangerous, intense,
days some young tough sheriff might have staked out
had he known their plots and secrets:
that armed bitter Sunday, smoking by his
liquor cache in the woods,
the doomed rare bobcat across the creek
frozen in the sights of his cocked handgun;
that moody Friday night,
punkish desperado high on Meigs County Gold,
running the rusted-out ridges at fifty-five
with his jailbait girl from Jericho,
a waif of blonde booze and smoke;
that bleak November-souled unsuccessful suicide,
gassing his chainsaw Thursday midnight
and staggering toward the neighbors;
or worst, the thirty silver days
of brilliant awful light
in which the high woods
his friend once kept in West Virginia
lay stunned
then pushed aside,
dynamite and dozer stripping off the top,
its driver shouting Elvis songs
above the snap and roar.

Message from Frackingport

Come quickly: the past huffs up
the borehole
and all the hills turn black.

Also in America

Also in America, Stupid often ran things:
the mayor of an air-blasting,
water-fouling steel town
who knew nothing of
falcons or vanishing shad;
the school administrator,
always indoors,
always hunched before her tiny computer
in her tiny room,
suppliant before the idol,
blinded by terabytes and spread sheets,
while outdoors, under
the freest, sun-charged sky,
a vast school garden went unplanted.

In America, Stupid was often in charge:
the bean-counter
who watched test scores
more closely than teachers
and students;
the technophile, looking to wire his school,
who declared a room full of books
"clutter,"
the ed-tech-biz operative
who sold her soul
to the maintenance of machines
and the eventual extinction
of teachers.

In America, Stupid often triumphed:
renewed bombing
to secure peace;
the bushhogged "eyesore"
weed-rich lot
reduced to naked soil
and finely-chopped trash
("we had to destroy the field
in order to mow it");
the neighborhood grocery,
fresh produce, fresh meat,
the only island in the food desert
of the 'hood,
credit to all,
free delivery to the aged,
family-run for fifty
years—closed by the State for a minor
food-stamp violation.

In America, Stupid often seduced:
showed its comely frame
to investors and traders of
mortgages;
offered moist incentives
for cutbacks in teachers
to meet the budget
while football
thrived at a loss;
handed out cakes and candy
to fast-fooded
diabetic children,
sold even more gizmos and couch-

based devices to keep
them unexercised and fat;
demolished farmland
for the installation of malls;
poisoned the night with
parking lot lamps;
shilled capital gains
and farmland losses—*Yes!*—
as clear progress toward
bigness and profit.

Not All Sides Are Represented Here

"Not all sides are
represented here,"
the quibblers, rabid capitalists, and
conscienceless would say,
"computers have more
up sides than down. War is always just.
Nuclear is necessary.
Coal can be clean.
"Points of view," they would say,
"will differ."
                  But the world,
the planet, did not reason,
did not equivocate;
it simply acted according
to its laws, most of which
they did not know—
for example, why so many
kinds of beetles? How much
smoke is too much?
Will oceans survive?
World was acted upon,
oftener and oftener,
by forces it could not
digest or comprehend:
2,000 new chemicals
every year, vast spills
of oil, billions of
fracking gallons poisoned and
lost to the water
cycle.

But there is not
an infinity of sides:
A box stops.
A diamond ends.
Cards flip once.
A world,
as we have seen,
can die.

Interrogation During The Old War

How large childhood remains
even after years of recollection,
vivid acreage without borders,
inhabited by infancy and boyhood.
Most everything was new then,
glint of skink or fence swift,
smell of copperheads,
the way a fire in the backyard oil drum
where we burned the trash
hissed and stank as it died.

*Was there no moment or question
that did not pry open a strange door?*

No, everything was new
as any of Emerson's gods of the days,
and every one wore new clothes, ribands of
stratocumulus, that new word that made the world
and my eyes new,
or stood beaded with tiger beetles quick as light
on the sand of the riverbank,
and the river itself, that recent
eater of a girl I loved, that giver
of catfish and shad,
that tormentor of snags and broken herons.

*Were there no repetitions beyond the wren's scales
sung in the yard every morning?*

Always—
and a cascade of vocabulary:
the day I learned *sperm,*
the day I learned *alibi,*
the days I chanted my altar boy Latin
and first pounded my chest
at the Confiteor:
Mea culpa, mea culpa, mea maxima culpa.

*Was there no end to verbiage, to saying, cursing, yelling,
praying, blabbing in the blab-school years
of times-tables and the names of presidents?*

Never: everywhere amid a rain of nouns,
stabbed and urged and soothed by avalanches of verbs,
tilted off-center by the adverb or strange adjective,
I reeled alive in words.

Only much later
did I learn of and mourn
the slaughters forwarded by politicians,
the confoundings that would not answer reason's call,
the outrages unjustified and unimpugned,
the skull-like grinning silences of war,
the dear, many, tongue-tied dead.

In The Time Of Great Extinctions

In his sixty-second year,
having made gardens
since he was fourteen,

he planted deep along his street
a post and sign: *Erie Gardens,*
the act of naming his pledge of permanence.

Now, three harvests have come to his hands
and gone out among neighbors
and customers—compatriots

in the alliances Wendell Berry calls for—
with light, rain, earth, work, and air,
those "Worthies."

If it is given to him to live
here another twenty years,
he hopes to do so in sweat and labor

under a calming sun, on a planet
made more healthful by proper use.
Let him not fear that trouble will surround him,

that the clouds he looks for with rain
will be the smoke of ruined lands and cities,
that a bitter ash will fall some day

and poison to death all that he has done.

Unfinished To Do List

—Name the illness:
   what makes us
   spoil the world
   for our great
   grandchildren?
   What makes us deaf
   to the alarums
   of weather and the land?

—Find the center of peace
   and live there
   like the chipmunks
   and the voles.

—Entertain light
   and air. Develop
   and deploy
   small factories
   of silence.

—Sing like a bee
   on a golden wire.

—Find three years
   in which to research
   on the wing
   and then write
   the long-suppressed,
   though long-needed
   *History of the World
   According to the Birds.*

STATES OF THE ARTS

The Poem's Work: After Salman Rushdie

The poem's work is to witness
all crucifixions, holocausts, and mass
suicides, and at the time
to note as calmly
and accurately as possible
the weather, crops, state of the birds.
During the train wreck,
the poem is to listen for music.
After the battle,
the poem is to polish,
as perfectly as possible,
the love letters of the dead.
Before Judgment Day,
the poem is to have written
all the decisions, hung the jurors,
set the defendants free.

During red, blue, and purple,
the poem is to load rapidly the brushes.

Following every marriage, every inauguration,
the poem is to assist in consummation.

Squash Erotic

My vegetable love should grow vaster than empires....
—Andrew Marvell

Is that a pistol in your pocket, or are you just happy to see me?
—Mae West

As if embare-assed-sad-but-wiser Adam
were remembered in its green genes,
zucchini attempts to hide
under a wide innocent leaf,
but can't help itself, nocturnally
quintuples, stiff and
monstrous.
Gadzukes! It swells imperially,
huge, blunt,
formidable, a blusher,
clunkily obstreperous,
annunciating its gorged jade burst.
Daily, Dawn's light touch
turns it on. Even language
pumps tumescent
in its presence.   But of course:
libido clones so many forms like this,
obelisks, towers, nozzles spewing diesel,
or butter, or lippy smooth soft-serve,
or geysers and volcanoes,
or hypnotic cobras
climbing from tight-woven baskets,
or upright gods erect at the edges
of old Roman fields, even

the blunt but potent
little bullets plugging road signs
out in the shires and counties,
seeding the whole August air
with wild reports, fecund echoes,
randy ricochets,
while swarped and bedazed amoretti
in garden-side hot caravans and trailers
writhe with sweet screams and groans
so that summer grows immense
with all that comes.

Elegy For
Before, Behind, Between, Above, Below
after Donne's "On His Mistress Going To Bed"

This is good: you, the pious clergyman,
doing it as us randy lesser men must do: omnivorous,
explorative, privateer of desire, the Drake
of her several oceans, alpinist
of her upthrust whitenesses,
excited skater-of-edges,
hand-spanning her silken reaches,
her thatched shires,
her musky fingerling precincts.

And better: she, inviting,
cave, strand, sheaves of unfolded linen,
moist purse gorged with gems and treasure,
she, open as the ocean to the oceanographer,
awash with consummatory tides
(which God has blessed and smiles upon),
and heaving against the shores
of you her naked wild beauty,
her moaning holy siren's song
in your delighted shipwrecked ear—

Oh, Donne—
body's world, the life
you made of love,
compassed and encompassing,
part and whole, onenesses

conceiving and conceived—
unmapped is the map, and lost
the lovely way:

Oh, Donne,
done.

After The Admonitions

Long ago, the local Yahweh,
Monsignor O'Shea, made it clear
(along with his icy coven of nuns)
that the body was for work,
the temple of Christ the Carpenter
and Fisher of Men, and that pleasure
and desire were two sides
of the same sin.

So when, by accident, I
brushed Karen Ormsby's
plush bottom, and she looked straight
at me and smiled,
all was lost.

To hell with fishing, with hammers
and saws: quickly came
sticky engagements,
tumbling sweet amalgamations,
then eventual skin-to-skins
in long August afternoons
when her dad was at work in the mill:
even as I burned with it,
I knew I would burn for it.

But our lips were torches, our groins
lighted gasoline, our palms
engulfed in gloves of flame;
wherever we touched,
we reignited, flared,

cried out, fell back—
exhausted on a blanket
that smelled of cats, wrenches,
sweat.
                And even when she'd pull down her skirt,
fix her hair, it was the beginning
of the next times: moist futures
promised new kinds
of slick joinery, dovetailing bodies,
nail-clinching embraces,
long, supple sessions of gathering up flush
engorgement and abandon,
the taut nets of our bodies
swashing with slick undulations
heavy, wet as any heaving seas.

Buenos Noches, Noches

You, black anxious blankness,
void interrupted by moments
of Imax panic,
you, the numb parentheses
around my restless dread, farewell.
Sleep, I kiss you
goodbye.
        And as you leave
my bedroom forever, I see
your drop your velvet
gown, smell the pale lilac
of your presence,
touch again in memory the silk
lassitude of your hips.
How empty my narrow bed now,
not even the roots of seedling
dreams entering my skin.

All day is now barren all day,
and all night is all night,
empty.

Sleep, the trains are stopped
in the tunnel, the moon
stalled behind a cloud,
the very word that means you
struck down in a
vacant hallway,
the doors all closed,
not even the slightest bloodstain
troubling the floor.

The Professor Eats a Late Linguine

She sucks (he observes)
the lean
strands slowly through
pursed lips,
puckered as if in
kissing. Sauce
stains lip skin—
it reddens as with lip-
stick. Then, partly sated,
she smiles, swallows,
sips her lip-red
wine, washing her
pasta down, lips
and tongue and
throat at work
as would be, eating
linguine, any sauced
saucy linguist's.

Acme Dream Removal

Whatever gorgeous technicolors
flood your dreams, Acme hauls them away
to a graveyard in black and white,
their hoopdie front-loader whining as it backs,
beeping like a rusty roadrunner.

Your moist encounter
with the prince, his wine and caviar, his
careful undressing of you into his arms
is there, become a scene from
the worst movie in a decade;
all your embraces now grapple ghosts
of virtuals you wasted last week
in your shrieking video game.

And that strange journey into the ocean
last Tuesday, after midnight,
your body blue and limber
as a wave, the taste of sea like honey
to your skin—

Gone, too, *kaput*, drained
like a baby pool into a suburban yard
littered with cocktail napkins, school vouchers,
blood-stained chadless ballots.

Everything—your diamond-eyed beau
with breath like a poppy field
and hands like pleasure all over,
your lost youth recovered like a body

made of light, all your secret
desires—health, good looks, money, heaven,
laid out like a banquet
before you, to enjoy—

All gone, hauled away by Acme and his belching partner
in his grubby wife-beater, his beard like
a slap of grease across his face:
between Acme and his man
even your sweetest pilgrims of youth
hunch like gut-loose drunks
in line for heaving Port-O-Lets.

Vlad

Albright recounted her impressions of Putin as the first senior U.S. official to meet him after he became Russia's president. She said she had noted at the time that he was "small and pale" and "so cold as to be almost reptilian."
—The New York Times

Another lizard claims its home
inside a human.
As if hunting flies,
it stretches its reasons for war
like a throat,
hungry.
It does not deliberate; it only eats—
the hands of old people,
the eyes of yellow cats,
the vertebrae of burnt houses.
It remembers back
through explosions
to its ancestors, before
the asteroid.
It believes its survival
is entitled,
not a splinter of luck.
It raises on its back,
like Dimetrodon, the sails
it will make its navies of,
the fans with which
it will whisk away
ashes, deep ashes, of its guilt.
It shows its salmon tongue.
It basks in a counterfeit sun

to power its invention of history
and insists the story
is a plant
it planted.

Alternative Facts: The Primer

The toad is warm-blooded
in the presence of the new Constitution,
and laws appear as strange lights over Kansas.
Magic is real.
In the presence of the new Constitution
even words may change: this is their nature,
as with axolotl or caterpillar.
We know that nouns—static, stable, touchable—
may transform into verbs with mottled feathers,
or grow camouflage that allows them to disappear
into their backgrounds. Know that
the groundhog, under special circumstances,
may fly.
        And so let not your heart be troubled:
though Little Black Sambo
may flee and flee and flee
he too will at last melt into sweetness
like honey or butter. All the chasing tigers
around him are angels. Ignore the teeth.
Declare away the teeth.
They will be gone, I tell you—
they will not be teeth.
They are not even tigers.

Come On

with apologies to Robert Browning

I have yuge ambitions—
big as my hands and junk, you know—
and I know you know
I know, Miss Pretty.
So just come over here
and sit down where my palm
can cover that knee of yours,
a fine thing, babe,
a warm starting place. We'll discuss payment
later, after some Red Bull and Cheezits.
If you look out
that window, you will see
one tower, just a bauble, really,
I've got six or seven like that
all over. But buildings are
boring, after all, and what
better thing to do than to
avoid being bored, the
old way of being unbored,
the old slap and tickle;
now you may
undress. Don't worry about
creases, I have a maid, the best ever,
young, Ukrainian, still
a virgin, can you believe it?
Later, downstairs, we'll
watch some Fox news
and I'll tweet a bit
and you can pick out a bracelet

from the box on the table,
thought a great thing,
which Jake of Brooklyn
pounded out of tin for me.

STEPS IN DEFENDING ONE'S SELF FROM "EMPOWERED IGNORANCE"

1.
Gather the facts
from impeccable sources
and array them with style,
logic, and beauty.

2.
Approach the opponent
with respect. Speak
calmly. Resist
firmly when
interrupted.

3.
Check everyone
for weapons.

4.
Remember all
the kind untruths
your mother told you
to keep your happiness
untrammeled.

5.

Remember that same
smiling, pleasant woman,
smelling of your breakfast
cinnamon, kept you
happy.

6.

Now, expect blatant unmotherly
denial of your points,
followed by public expressions
of scorn and contempt.

7.

Do not appeal
to reason when it is clear
that reason does not prevail.

8.

Shorten that to RDNP
and expect to encounter it
again and again.

9.

Swallow your anger.

10.

Stifle your outrage.

11.

Order out for a massage.

12.
Practice the pangolin
defense:
roll up into a
ball and close
your eyes.

13.
After the "bargaining
session" breaks down
and the taunting foe, tucking
in his napkin,
calls for cheeseburgers and a Coke,

check everyone, again,

for guns.

What Suits, You?

The plaid flannel of the boy next door
says "Millennial," along with the beard
and the old briar pipe. Signs of the times.

So what to make of the suits
in Washington, their narrow
palettes of blues and grays,
their fat bright ties
like front windows in Las Vegas?
And what about their aides and secretaries,
their strangling conservative ensembles,
their tight-waisted monochrome numbers
with the poopsie labels "Kayleigh"
or "Kellyanne"?

Never once have I seen
in foreground or background
on TV from the Capitol
a man in a stained t-shirt and blue-jeans,
hair slicked back, a pack of Luckies
rolled into his shirt sleeves,
pushing a necessary broom.

He's my kind of guy, fellow citizen,
someone out of Steubenville
in the 1950s, his dad a buddy of Dino's,
his slick uncle Guido
transparently, straightforwardly mean,
an equal access felon,
and well-spoken as any high-end crook
that we will ever see,
President Company included.

The Capitol Grill

After the coals were lit
by singing caucuses of nuns and teachers

and the embers glowed as red
as rage, or embarrassment,

they mixed the Honesty Rub—
lie-dried facts shed daily

from Kellyanne Conway,
coarse Graham-crackered dusts,

chopped McConnell-peppered stallings—
to raise the heat on all the serious grilling.

Soon, the President answered questions
about climate change,

admitting that the floors of forests
cannot be swept, however yuge the broom.

Soon, the Vice President conceded
that his wife is not his mother,

despite his calling her that.
Soon, popping and wheezing

like sausages over a hot spot,
covid false counselors resigned,

lizardly senators retired early,
seared cabinet members fled in bulky Russian sedans,

and the smoke over American backyards
formed clouds of willing surrender,

cumuli of abject apologies,
whole happy cyclones of justice and kumbaya.

Hurt God

> *"…take away your guns, destroy your Second Amendment, no religion, no anything, hurt the Bible, hurt God."*
> —45's claims about what Democrats will do, Cleveland, August 6, 2020

She shambles past Golgotha,
remembering bitter times.
In her mouth, her own blood
still tastes of iron nails.
She hasn't voted yet,
but plans to,
that revenge,
that anti-insurrection.
That resurrection.

Beautiful

"We won two world wars, two world wars, beautiful wars that were vicious and horrible."
—Donald J. Trump

"Brand new beautiful equipment ..."
—on munitions he would send to Iran

"There is something beautiful about that, when you're watching everybody get pushed around, there's something very beautiful about that."
—on violent law-enforcement at Minnesota protests

As the bones of Anzio were beautiful.
As the Western Front was beautiful.
As our grandfathers' wounds in Belgium were beautiful.
As the banzai attacks on Saipan were beautiful.
As Hamburger Hill was beautiful, and Khe San, and Ia Drang were beautiful.

As the blood under the sky of Gettysburg was beautiful.
As the drowned children along the border are beautiful.
As the poisoning of the rivers is beautiful.
As the tear-gassing of protestors is beautiful.

As the knee on the neck is beautiful.
As the years in Guantanamo are beautiful.
As the maskless in crowds are beautiful.
As the covid burials are beautiful.

As the AK-47 is beautiful.
As the methane leaks are beautiful.
As the wildfires are beautiful.
As any very stable genius: beautiful.

Soup To Nuts

This is not a Marx Brothers
routine: no forging of words
into a slapstick of puns,
nor a wacky alchemical display,
bouillabaisse into Cracker Jack.

From soup to nuts
now means, in our world
of alternative facts,
that porridge may be steak,
a president might be a liar and thief,
that discussions once focused,
deliberated, and concluded
are now blendered willynilly
into blather and partisan froth.

Soup to nuts—
used to be a kind of catch-all
notion, a sort of encyclopedia
of courses, the unfolding of
what and how much, but now it's

whatever   lol

vague semi-factoids
like electrons knocked out of orbit
and headed in all directions
like the hair of a clown
who stands in a bathtub of gin,
holding a naked live wire.

Linnaeus Sniffs Around The Capital

> *Carolus Linnaeus…proposed seven basic scent classes: aromatic, fragrant, musky, garlicky, repulsive, nauseous, and goaty."*
> —NYT *This Day In History*: Feb. 22,'83: "Sense of Smell Proves to be Surprisingly Subtle"

Repulsive

At first the press conferences
smelled like smoke-filled back rooms,
crowded and unruly, but effective.
Notebook pages fluttered
like albino eagles.
Pens wrote for miles
about taxes and race and dead rivers.

Now, there is no destination at all,
just the smell of empty chairs
—which is the smell of funerals—
and far-off down a maze of dim hallways,
cheap coffee burning on a hotplate.

Aromatic

Deceptive, it insinuates itself through
the air conditioners of Congress, rises from the urinals
of the Executive Offices, scents even the
lobbies of the Dept. of Agriculture, where it is
misrepresented as "bees and honey." As with diesel fumes,
some find it pleasant. It carries, however,
dangers of many kinds: suffocation, diminished cognition,
verbal slip-ups, a tendency toward blather. Like the

flowers of Rappacini, though it seems
beautiful, it kills. "Breathe among these beauties,"
then dead: you die.

Fragrant

No, not "flagrant," through
there is much of that,
enough to set off the soul's smoke alarms.
What happens daily smells like alewives
rotting ashore, shoals of minnows
poisoned below the power plant,
dead heifers swelling in a West Virginia meadow.
Dark waters smell so, and the first three circles of hell,
even the moldy ruins of some warehouse
full of a million spoiled American apple pies.

Musky

A sort of sharper moldiness,
not exactly musty but close: just one letter off.
Imagine the smoke as ham burns and burns
in a skillet. This is called filibuster.
Think of the overloaded sump below a flock
of migrants' trailers. This is called governing.
Imagine grandmother locked in her own
fruit cellar, long-rotten peaches
sticky on the shelves. Potatoes with
gouged-out eyes. Imagine crowded down there,
shoulder to shoulder, unwashed caucuses of men
in shabby suits counting stolen ballots
and laughing. This is called
victory.

Garlicky

Hours later, after the acquittal,
it still lives on the breath of Congress
so that you turn your head away, blinking.
It is like an anti-perfume: *take that, you beautiful republic.*
It is cloven, like the devil's hooves.
It is underground, like that exile, righteousness.
It is overwhelming, scenting everything
like a smashed skunk in the aisles
of the Senate, or the stink of bushfires,
a whole ignited Oregon approaching Pennsylvania
Avenue,
storming in on all sides.

Nauseous

Like a bad paraphrase of Amendments to the
Constitution,
it sickens the whole populace. Hands with which
to sign last-minute, prophylactic bills suddenly fall off.
Consciences explode like beaten piñatas.
Curb-side drains emit gray clouds of legislation.
Restraints on pollution are waved as the skies
darken with fracking mist. Lungs fill
with radium. The eyes of newborns
glow a neon green, and milk is banned,
along with the mothers who produce it.

Goaty

This is the most characteristic of all: a stink that feeds on
anything—pointed lies, dull misinformation, fanged

and aggressive stupidity. It chews
the cracking bones of the state. Citizens
can smell it—bad barnyard, swill with bloated pigs,
coops of dead hens. Good ideas lie everywhere
under mounds of fresh earth while government
undertakers purse their lips and count their dollars.
Theirs is the most expanding
work in the economy. Congratulations
are thrown at their feet and become dead rabbits.
Seasoned with paper and stale legislation, soups simmer
on the stoves of Washington,
a stiff flipped bird—an eagle—in every pot.

America

> *America is a strange man*
> *lying in a wheatfield.*
> —Robert Sund

He has come
a long and unknown way,
a great ingot of gold
glowing behind his
eyes. He speaks to no one
because he knows
everyone will make up,
on their own,
his story. Some will be
full of proud blood
and seized lands.
Some will be
overrun with dirty money and
steel mills. Some will
confess to unforgivable
sins against water
and land. Some will deny
everything, casting the blame off
on the poor, the homeless,
on the demands of profit,
on the unrelenting obligations
of politics and greed—
or on those who speak foreign
tongues. All of these stories
will be well-reported,
wired to the farthest reaches
of the empire,

promulgated even unto the high,
private places where the suit-gods
reign in grim silence.
And some will be so
true they will go
unnoticed for centuries,
acknowledged far too late
to fix anything that's
wrong.

Marshal Law

> *A Republican who urged the Trump White House to declare martial law to stop Joe Biden taking office has only one regret: that he misspelled "martial"*

No problem, sir:
we know who you meant.
The one in the tall hat, in from the saloon
from *Gunsmoke*: his dusty Stetson,
his brassy corset of ammo,
the never-smile frozen on his face.
Here he needs no gimpy sidekick,
just a tongueless AR-15
loyal at his side,
gleaming in whiskied light.
He arranges and rearranges
his hat brim
instead of talking,
closes his eyes when spoken to.
His fists are veined grenades.

When the first round is served, he
shoots. After the smoke clears
he shouts. No one knows
what he's saying. Eventually,
though, everyone marches,
magazines and holsters
helter-skeltered across the floor
as after a mass shooting
or tornado.

It's he they have called
to make their plans go well,
the cops overrun, patriots
stabbing with flags, the good
old boys, those tough Dan'l Boones,
bear-spraying their way into history.

The Inevitability Of Sand

Outside the small, all that is large prances and parades. It elephants, it whales, it wildebeests and stampedes, raising clouds of dust everywhere it goes. "Look at me," all that is large shouts, with its beery breath like an engineer's laid off for weeks. "Look at me," it shouts, "I am all that is large, I am truck, ship, tower, greed, debt, Texas. Step aside!" Meanwhile, small keeps to itself in its house no larger than a bean. Among pieces of bone, hair, thimbles, small chuckles to itself, reading the paper's headlines, which are all about all that is large. "It's just a matter of time," small mutters, folding the pages with a wise smile. "Then all will be mine."

Pilgrims

Failing To Make It To The New Frontier

They settle in anonymous utopias

near the outerbelt, close to sports malls,
furniture outlets, putt-putt courses

not far from the ruins of abandoned small towns

where the churches are now warehouses
for discontinued Christmas items

and the mayor's into blondes and real estate

in Florida and the grade school has been
abandoned too and a new one put up,

multiple-building style in the middle of a field.

No trees. High fence.

It looks like barracks, grassless boot camp,
except for the cute swings by the parking lot.

Fifteen Mile Drive To School

Past two or three hundred places
whose names and stories are lost.

Where once a barn shone, full of calves.

Where three willows let their hair down over lovers
weeping in a gully.

Where two hundred eighteen years ago a bear walked,
and someone cocked a rifle.

Now it's algebra, keyboarding, or the only
events that even remember the word "field":

football, hockey.

Driving Drunk In The Subdivision

No one prays, or even imagines
to pray, that he might make
the right turn
at the place where
he usually goes wrong.

No one prays or imagines
that he might drive
off the edge
of that new nowhere,

out of the subdivision
with its expensive starter
castles and drifts
of mulch, and come home
closer to the woods of history:

there the creek warbles past
a quiet corn field
where every ear listens to
its roots, gone sweet
on the good old news.

Conduit

after a metaphor for the poet by Octavio Paz

Ears are torn off, tongues jerked out,
villages poisoned, cities fouled, but

I am waiting as an empty pipe waits.
Far off, in mountains where people speak

pidgin-hijacked languages, it is daily fire.
Children toss dolls and burning rags in ditches.

Birds enflame small trees. Near and far,
narrow creeks begin to rise and testify.

Every leaf in the rainy forest is a highway down
for truth's vivid rivulets.

Below a stone dam built long ago
by boys already dead, I gather and I hear.

I am wide, long-lived as water, many-eared.
Listen! Soon I fill, and sing.

NOTES

"Xenia"
The setting at the beginning of this poem is Over-The-Rhine, a now-gentrified downtown district of Cincinnati formerly the destination for displaced Appalachian out-migrants and urban African Americans. It is where the events that are featured in "Riot" in *Public Hearings* took place. "All pale forms fainting at the door" is taken from the deeply empathetic Stephen Foster song "Hard Times," published in 1854. Foster lived for a time on the riverfront at Cincinnati.

"How Long Ago The Heat"
I acknowledge the imagery of the fine children's book, *No Star Nights* by Anna Egan Smucker, friend and fellow Steubenville, Ohio native.

"Afternoon With Young Poet"
The embedded dragonfly haiku is by Issa, the Japanese poet who lived from 1762-1828. "In a Station of the Metro" is by Ezra Pound.

"What Suits, You"
Kellyanne Conway was 45's Senior Counselor. On *6/13/2019* The U.S. Office of Special Counsel (OSC) sent a report to President Donald J. Trump finding that Counselor to the President Kellyanne Conway violated the Hatch Act on numerous occasions by disparaging Democratic presidential candidates while speaking in her official capacity during television interviews and on social media. —U.S Office of Special Counsel. She was the inventor and purveyor of what she termed "alternative facts."

Kayleigh McEnany
45's Press Secretary. On May 1, 2020, as part of her first public press briefing and the first one by a White House press secretary in 417 days, McEnany was asked by an Associated Press reporter: "Will you pledge to never lie to us from that podium?" McEnany replied: "I will never lie to you. You have my word on that." On the subject of Trump's responses to the coronavirus pandemic, she redundantly claimed, "This president has always sided on the side of data."—*Wikipedia*

"In Vivid Sunlight, Becca"
Heraclitus was a Greek philosopher who, among other things, claimed all things were made of fire.

"Resistance, Or Our Most Worthy Habits"
The Supreme Court says it won't review the conviction of former coal CEO Don Blankenship, who was found guilty of conspiring to violate safety standards at West Virginia's Upper Big Branch mine before the 2010 explosion that killed 29 men. https://apnews.com/article/us-supreme-court-decisions-coal-mining-don-blankenship-government-and-politics-b4883d6e899f989b229a1600285fd4f3

"Marshal Law"
This is the second of two infamous spelling errors that exist for me like a set of mocking parentheses around the misrule of the 45th President. First, Secretary of Education Betsy DeVos's misspelling of W.E.B. Du Bois, for which she then posted a follow-up post headed "Deepest Apologizes," and then this, by Congressman Ralph Norman of South Carolina.

"Outbreaks"
"I worry that students are losing the ability to make eye contact and read body language, and that they are not being prepared to be effective citizens, workers, and family members. This disconnect from in-person communication also relates to a distance from the natural world, and a growing indifference to the destruction of our environment. In this alienation from nature and natural environments, people, also lose the ability to distinguish between true and false representations. Since on the web, everything is a virtual image or simulation generated by digital code, we live in a state of constant in-difference." —Bob Samuels, *"Being Present: A Critique of OnLine Learning"* https://ucaft.org/content/being-present-critique-online-education-bob-samuels

"Not All Sides Are Represented Here"
Number of chemicals introduced each year: https://www.pbs.org/newshour/science/it-could-take-centuries-for-epa-to-test-all-the-unregulated-chemicals-under-a-new-landmark-bill
Water waste in fracking: See https://www.nrdc.org/stories/fracking-101

"Come On"
See Robert Browning's "My Last Duchess."

"Beautiful"
wars: *Independent* 20 July 2020
equipment: *https://www.outlookindia.com/website/story/world-news-will-send-brand-new-beautiful-equipment-if-iran-donald-trumps-fresh-warning/345191*
pushed around: *TMZ* 18 October 2020

"Conduit"
As a witness poet might "sing"—that is, testify as to what has been seen.

ABOUT THE AUTHOR

RICHARD HAGUE, a native of Steubenville, Ohio in the Appalachian Ohio River Valley, taught at Purcell Marian High School in Cincinnati for 45 years. While there he engaged in other enterprises and adventures, including adjuncting at Edgecliff College and at Xavier University, his alma mater, commercial urban gardening, hosting writers workshops, and teaching for a few summers at the Institute for Professional Development and Graduate School of Education at Northeastern University in Boston. His high school career ended when he refused to sign an anti-gay and anti-worker's rights Archdiocese of Cincinnati contract in May 2014. Not long after, he was named Writer-in-Residence at Thomas More University in northern Kentucky, where he continued as Artist-in-Residence until 2022. He now teaches and writes with The Originary Arts Initiative. He is author, co-editor, or editor of 20 collections, most recently *Riparian: Poetry, Short Prose and Photography Inspired by the Ohio River* (Dos Madres Press, 2019), *Earnest Occupations: Teaching, Writing, Gardening & Other Local Work* (Bottom Dog Press, 2018), *Studied Days: Poems Early & Late in Appalachia* (Dos Madres Press, 2017), *Where Drunk Men Go: A Long Poem* (Dos Madres Press, 2015) and *During The Recent Extinctions: New &*

Selected Poems 1984-2012 (Dos Madres Press), for which he was given the Weatherford Award in Poetry. Other books include *Milltown Natural: Essays and Stories from a Life* (Bottom Dog Press, 1997), nominated for a National Book Award, the poetry collections *Alive in Hard Country* (Bottom Dog Press, 2003), named 2003 Poetry Book of the Year by the Appalachian Writers Association, *Ripening* (The Ohio State University Press, 1984), for which he was named Co-Poet of the Year in Ohio in 1985, and *Lives of the Poem: Community & Connection in a Writing Life* (Wind Publications, 2005) a multi-genre memoir, poetry collection, and teaching handbook. In 1994, The literature and writing Program he designed at Purcell Marian High School received the First Place, United States of America, "Excellence In Teaching English" Award, Native-Speaking Category, from the English-Speaking Union. He has been a Finalist for The Bechtel Prize from *Teachers & Writers*, the AWP Award in Creative Nonfiction, The Pablo Neruda Prize from *Nimrod*, The Iowa Prize in Nonfiction, and a Bob Costas Writing Award. He continues to live in Cincinnati.

Author photo by Scott Goebel

ACKNOWLEDGMENTS

Thanks to the editors of the following:

"Catiary" appeared in *Pegasus*

"Where Are They And What Are They Doing There?" appeared in *Sheila-Na-Gig*

"To Kiss A Train" and "Men At Work" appeared in *Pine Mt. Sand & Gravel*

"In The Time of Great Extinctions" and "Industrious" and "Landscape, Near the End" and "Finger: an Elegy in Eights" and "Nevertheless, Wonders" and "Message From Frackingport" and "How Long Ago The Heat" appeared in *Still: The Journal*

"The Professor Eats A Late Linguine" appeared in *Journal of Kentucky Studies*

"Characters For a Novel of The Days" appeared in *New Southerner* 2014 Literary Edition

"Virginity" appeared in *ABZ Poetry Press*

"What Suits, You?" and "What is Worse" appeared *in Northern Appalachia Review*

"Covid Diary" appeared in *A 21st Century Plague: Poetry from a Pandemic* ed. Elayne Clift, University Press Publishers 2021

"*Ab Sum*" and "Elegy for *Before, Behind, Between, Above, Below* appeared in *Smartish Pace*

"Song For St. Survivor" appeared in *The Poet's Craft*, blog of the Poet Laureate of Cincinnati

"HELL IS REAL" appeared in *Iron Mountain Review* Vol. XXX Fall 2015, Richard Hague Issue

"Resistance, Or, Our Most Worthy Habits" appeared in *Appalachian Reckoning: A Region Responds to* Hillbilly Elegy. eds. Meredith McCarroll and Anthony Harkins, West Virginia University Press 2019

"The Capitol Grill" and "Alternative Facts: The Primer" and "The Tranquility Trials" and "Xenia" and "Limitlesss" and "Conduit" and "Steps In Defending One's Self from Willful Ignorance" and "Pilgrims" and "Unfinished To Do List" and "Not All Sides Are Represented Here" and "Irrecoverable, Or The Long War" and "America" appeared in various editions of *For A Better World: Poems of Peace & Justice,* ed. Saad Ghosn, Cincinnati, OH.

"Linnaeus Sniffs Around The Capital" appeared in *Gyroscope Review*

"Vlad" appeared in *Quiet Diamonds,* Orchard Street Press

Other books by Richard Hague
published by Dos Madres Press

Burst—Poems Quickly (2004)

During the Recent Extinctions
New & Selected Poems 1984-2012 (2012)

Where Drunk Men Go (2015)

Beasts, River, Drunk Men, Garden, Burst, & Light
sequences and long poems (2016)

Studied Days
Poems Early & Late in Appalachia (2017)

He is also Editor of:
Realms of the Mothers:
The First Decade of Dos Madres Press - 2016

For the full Dos Madres Press catalog:
www.dosmadres.com

Printed by Libri Plureos GmbH in Hamburg, Germany